Editor
Gisela Lee, M.A.

Managing Editor
Karen Goldfluss, M.S. Ed.

Editor-in-Chief
Sharon Coan, M.S. Ed.

Cover Artist
Barb Lorseyedi

Art Coordinator
Kevin Barnes

Art Director
CJae Froshay

Imaging
Ralph Olmedo, Jr.

Product Manager
Phil Garcia

Publisher
Mary D. Smith, M.S. Ed.

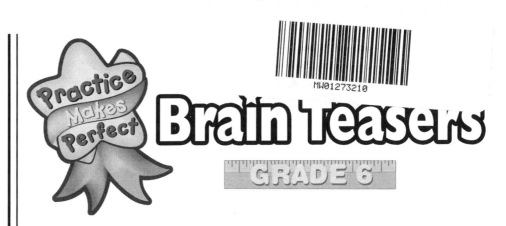

Practice Makes Perfect Brain Teasers
GRADE 6

Author

Mary Rosenberg

Teacher Created Resources, Inc.
6421 Industry Way
Westminster, CA 92683
www.teachercreated.com

ISBN: 978-0-7439-3756-6

©2003 Teacher Created Resources, Inc.
Reprinted, 2013
Made in U.S.A.

Table of Contents

Introduction

The old adage "practice makes perfect" can really hold true for your child and his or her education. The more practice and exposure your child has with concepts being taught in school, the more success he or she is likely to find. For many parents, knowing how to help your children can be frustrating because the resources may not be readily available. As a parent it is also difficult to know where to focus your efforts so that the extra practice your child receives at home supports what he or she is learning in school.

This book has been designed to help parents and teachers reinforce basic skills with children. *Practice Makes Perfect* reviews basic math skills for children in grade 6. This book contains 39 brain teasers that allow children to learn, review, and reinforce math concepts. Brain teasers have long proven their worth as vehicles of learning. Such activities carry with them curiosity and delight. While it would be impossible to include all concepts taught in grade 6 in this book, the following basic objectives are reinforced through the brain teasers:

- word problems
- logic and reasoning
- graphing
- time
- money
- basic geometry
- number patterns/sequences and exponential numbers

- subtraction
- addition
- multiplication
- division
- basic algebra
- factorials, combinations, and permutations
- using charts and other graphics

How to Make the Most of This Book

Here are some useful ideas for optimizing the activity pages in this book:

- Set aside a specific place in your home to work on the activity pages. Keep it neat and tidy with materials on hand.
- Set up a certain time of day to work on the brain teasers. This will establish consistency. Look for times in your day or week that are less hectic and more conducive to practicing skills.
- Keep all practice sessions with your child positive and constructive.
- Help with instructions, if necessary. If your child is having difficulty understanding what to do or how to get started, work through the first problem with him or her.
- Review the work your child has done. This serves as reinforcement and provides further practice.
- Allow your child to use whatever writing instruments he or she prefers. For example, colored pencils can add variety and pleasure to the activity page.
- Pay attention to the areas in which your child has the most difficulty. Provide extra guidance and exercises in those areas.
- Look for ways to make real-life applications to the skills being reinforced.

Brain Teaser 1

What's the Order of Operations?

Directions: Using multiplication and division, solve the problems below. Remember, you can only use multiplication and division. The first one is done for you as an example.

1.	1 x 9 x 8 ÷ 12 = 6
2.	15 15 5 9 3 = 15
3.	56 4 7 2 = 4
4.	156 4 2 2 = 156
5.	635 6 10 3 = 127
6.	77 11 8 14 = 4
7.	25 60 10 15 = 10
8.	72 8 9 4 6 = 54
9.	145 5 4 2 = 232
10.	8460 10 94 2 = 18

Brain Teaser 2

Unscramble the Numbers

Directions: For each problem unscramble the dividend and/or the divisor to find the given quotient. The first one is done for you as an example.

1.	$414 \div 12 = 12$ ⟶	$144 \div 12 = 12$
2.	$661 \div 41 = 44$ ⟶	
3.	$913 \div 92 = 11$ ⟶	
4.	$753 \div 51 = 25$ ⟶	
5.	$594 \div 15 = 63$ ⟶	
6.	$2765 \div 64 = 56$ ⟶	
7.	$0390 \div 026 = 15$ ⟶	
8.	$2179 \div 91 = 19$ ⟶	
9.	$9849 \div 17 = 69$ ⟶	
10.	$5598 \div 939 = 15$ ⟶	

Brain Teaser 3 ⟁ ✺ ⟁ ✺ ⟁ ✺ ⟁ ✺ ⟁ ✺ ⟁ ⟁ ✺

Number Fun and Magic 3!

If you have difficulty solving some of these brain teasers, try drawing the problem. It often helps to picture what's being described.

Number Fun

1. Nancy and Bill ate breakfast at school. Bill ate five pancakes and Nancy ate two fewer than Bill. How many pancakes did Nancy eat? _____

2. Fred is two years older than Paul but six years younger than Bill. If Bill is 24, how old is Fred? _____ How old is Paul? _____

3. Mrs. Thomas baked two dozen cookies, but Tad ate eight of them. How many cookies did she have left? _____

4. Mr. O'Leary will cook for eight people on Sunday. If one cup of rice will feed four people, how many cups of rice will he need to cook for eight people? _____

5. If you divided an hour into four equal parts, what would you call each part? _____ How many minutes are there in each part? _____

Magic 3!

Steps	Sample
1. Choose a number.	58
2. Multiply by 3.	58 x 3 = 174
3. Add 1.	174 + 1 = 175
4. Add 1 again.	175 + 1 = 176
5. Now add the three answers you got in steps 2, 3, and 4.	174 + 175 + 176 = 525
6. Add the digits in the sum.	5 + 2 + 5 = 12
7. Keep adding the digits in each sum until a single digit is reached. This will always be 3.	1 + 2 = 3

Try this trick with numbers you choose. Show a friend. Say, "You may select any number that you like. If you do as I say, I will tell you the answer."

Brain Teaser 4

Strike It Rich!

Whose picture is on the $5,000 bill?

To discover the answer, find the difference in each problem below. Decode the name by matching the answer to its letter. Write the letter in the box below the difference.

9371	3313	7500	6000	6230
− 4528	− 1834	− 2627	− 3444	− 4985

☐ ☐ ☐ ☐ ☐

7927	7203	5361	7455	4079	8752	5386
− 3054	− 5724	− 3142	− 3679	− 2834	− 6273	− 2174

☐ ☐ ☐ ☐ ☐ ☐ ☐

1479	3776	4843
A	**I**	**J**
2219	4873	2556
D	**M**	**E**
3212	1245	2479
N	**S**	**O**

Brain Teaser 5 ᵔ ᕮ ᵔ ᕮ ᵔ ᕮ ᵔ ᕮ ᵔ ᵔ ᕮ

How Much Did They Eat?

Solve each problem.

1. Sue ate $2/4$ of an eight slice pizza.

   Sue ate _____ slices of pizza.

2. Bill ate $1/3$ of a 6 slice pie.

   Bill ate _____ slices of pie.

3. Gabby ate $1/4$ of a foot long hot dog.

   Gabby ate _____ inches of a foot long hot dog.

4. Bud ate $2/6$ of a dozen donuts.

   Bud ate _____ donuts.

5. Sam ate $2/3$ of a three layer cake.

   Sam ate _____ layers of a cake.

6. Brittany ate $1/2$ of a ten ounce box of candy.

   Brittany ate _____ ounces of candy.

7. Ivan ate $4/5$ of the 20 brownies.

   Ivan ate _____ brownies.

8. Cheryl ate $3/5$ of the 100 cinnamon candies.

   Cheryl ate _____ cinnamon candies.

9. $1/4$ of an octopus's legs divided by $1/2$ of a bird's legs.

   _____ legs

10. $1/5$ of the fingers on the left hand divided by $2/5$ of the fingers on the right hand.

    _____ fingers

11. $1/3$ of the legs of a tripod divided by $3/4$ of the legs on a coffee table.

    _____ legs

12. $1/10$ of the years in a century divided by $1/2$ of the years in a decade.

    _____ years

13. $1/6$ of a foot divided by $1/6$ of a yard.

    _____ inches

14. $1/12$ of the hours in one day divided by $1/12$ of the number of seconds in one minute.

    _____ minutes

15. $2/5$ of the sides of a pentagon divided by $1/4$ of the sides of a square.

    _____ sides

16. $5/6$ of the sodas in a 6 pack divided by $3/4$ of the sodas in a 12 pack.

    _____ sodas

Brain Teaser 6

Fraction Word Problems

Sample

Jerry ate $\frac{1}{4}$ of a cheese pizza and $\frac{1}{2}$ of a pepperoni pizza. How much pizza did he eat in all?

$$\frac{1}{4} = \frac{1}{4}$$
$$+ \frac{1}{2} = \frac{2}{4}$$
$$\overline{\quad\quad \frac{3}{4}}$$

Jerry ate $\frac{3}{4}$ of a pizza.

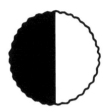

Directions: Compute the answers to these problems. Reduce your answers to lowest terms (that is, simplify your answer).

1. Your best friend ate $\frac{1}{3}$ of a lemon pie and $\frac{3}{6}$ of a chocolate pie. How much pie did your friend eat altogether? _____

2. Your principal bought $\frac{5}{6}$ of a pepperoni pizza and $\frac{7}{8}$ of a pineapple pizza. How much pizza did he buy in all? _____

3. At a birthday party, one child ate $\frac{2}{3}$ of a cake and another ate $\frac{1}{9}$ of the cake. How much more cake did the first child eat? _____

4. A third grader ate $\frac{2}{6}$ of a candy bar. A fourth grader ate $\frac{1}{2}$ of a candy bar. How much more candy did the fourth grader eat? _____

5. Albert bought $\frac{11}{12}$ of a pizza. Betty bought $\frac{5}{8}$ of a pizza. How much pizza did they buy altogether? _____

6. The fourth-grade teacher ate $\frac{1}{6}$ of a cake. The fifth grade teacher ate $\frac{1}{9}$ of a cake. How much more cake did the fourth-grade teacher eat? _____

7. The soccer coach had $\frac{9}{12}$ of a pizza. He gave the baseball coach $\frac{5}{9}$ of the pizza. How much pizza did the soccer coach have left? _____

Brain Teaser 7

Brain Teaser Potpourri

Cloud Cover

Help the weather forecaster explain what percent of the sky will be covered by clouds.

Type	Description	Write the Percentages
Clear	Sky has no clouds or clouds cover less than $\frac{1}{10}$ of the sky.	from 0 to 10%
Scattered	An average of $\frac{1}{10}$ to $\frac{5}{10}$ is covered.	
Broken	Clouds covered $\frac{5}{10}$ to $\frac{9}{10}$ of the sky.	
Overcast	Clouds covered $\frac{9}{10}$ of the sky.	

Thanksgiving Puzzle

Can you solve this Thanksgiving puzzle? **T** has been done for you. One of the letters is extra and does not belong in the puzzle.

___	___	___	___	___	___	T	___
0	**1**	**2**	**3**	**4**	**5**	**6**	**7**

1. T: It is a multiple of 2. It is greater than 4.
2. M: It is less than $(10 - 5)$. It is less than $T - 2$.
3. U: It is a multiple of 5. It is greater than M.
4. R = M + T − 1
5. Y: Divide T by M.
6. L: U x L = U
7. O: It is greater than T − M. It is less than 5.
8. H: H − O = M
9. P = U − U

Kite Factory

On a visit to a kite factory, Guadalupe noticed that the kites were made in the following repeated order: dragon, box, bat, fish, tiger, turkey. What will the design be on the 77th kite? _____

Brain Teaser 8

Number Puzzle #1

Write each number in the Number Puzzle.

6-Digit Numbers

121,109	310,454	410,228	539,975	951,414
227,116	334,107	461,061	638,720	956,637
288,109	358,123	461,597	876,674	958,861

Brain Teaser 9

Number Puzzle #2

Write each number in the Number Puzzle.

7-Digit Numbers

1,043,110	2,977,327	4,135,625	8,710,384
1,512,510	3,346,491	5,741,028	9,916,492
1,641,988	3,576,565	6,328,106	9,978,827

Brain Teaser 10

Brain Benders

Solve each number problem. *(Hint: Write the digits on sticky notes or small pieces of paper. Arrange the numbers to fit each set of clues.)*

1. Numbers to Use: 2, 8, 8
   - The 8s are not next to each other.
   - What is the number?

2. Numbers to Use: 6, 7, 9
   - It is an odd number.
   - The 9 is in between an odd and an even number.
   - The 7 is in the ones place.
   - What is the number?

3. Numbers to Use: 5, 6, 9
   - It is an even number.
   - The 5 has a greater value than the 9.
   - What is the number?

4. Numbers to Use: 1, 2, 2, 5
   - The two 2s are next to each other.
   - It is an even number.
   - The 5 has a value greater than both 2s but a lesser value than the 1.
   - What is the number?

5. Numbers to Use: 1, 1, 4, 8
   - It is an odd number.
   - The 4 is in between an odd digit and an even digit.
   - The 8 has the greatest value.
   - What is the number?

6. Numbers to Use: 1, 5, 7, 8
   - It is an even number.
   - The 1 has the greatest value.
   - The 5 has a value greater than the 7 but a lesser value than the 1.
   - What is the number?

Brain Teaser 11

More Brain Benders

Solve each number problem. (*Hint:* Write the digits on sticky notes or small pieces of paper. Arrange the numbers to fit each set of clues.)

1. Numbers to Use: 1, 1, 4, 8, 9
   - The 1s have the greatest and the least value.
   - The 9 has a greater value than both the 4 and a 1 and a lesser value than both the 8 and the other 1.
   - What is the number?

2. Numbers to Use: 1, 2, 3, 8, 9
   - It is an even number.
   - All of the odd numbers are next to each other. The even numbers are not next to each other.
   - The even numbers are in a sequence with the greater number first.
   - The odd numbers are in a sequence with the largest number first and the smallest number last.
   - What is the number?

3. Numbers to Use: 1, 2, 3, 3, 4
   - The two 3s are next to each other.
   - The 1 and 2 are next to each other.
   - The 4 and 2 are next to each other.
   - One of the 3s has the least value.
   - An even number has the greatest value.
   - What is the number?

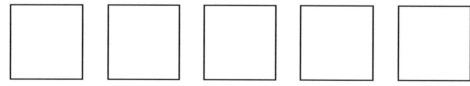

4. Numbers to Use: 1, 4, 5, 6, 7, 8, 9
   - The 1 has the greatest value. The 4 has the least value.
   - The 6 has a greater value than the 8 but a lesser value than the 1.
   - The 7 has a greater value than the 4 but a lesser value than the 5.
   - The 9 has a greater value than the 5 but a lesser value than the 8.
   - What is the number?

Brain Teaser 12

Tricky Averages

The **mean**, **median**, and **mode** are all verifiable averages. But sometimes one more clearly represents a set of data better than another.

Directions: Look at the data below. Calculate the mean, median, and mode. Consider the needs of each person's perspective. Then, decide which average is best.

Annual Job Salaries at One's Employer's Business

$30,000	$35,000	$30,000	$40,000	$37,000
$60,000	$48,000	$30,000	$40,000	$80,000

---

1. mean: _____   **2.** median: _____   **3.** mode: _____

4. If you were the employer trying to attract the best people to hire, which average would you list in a want ad? Why?_____

_____

5. If you were considering to come to work for this employer, which average salary would you like this company to tell you? Why? _____

_____

6. A toy company tells you the average cost of a specific kind of doll is $30. Your favorite aunt collects these dolls, and you wish to buy one for her. Do you hope this advertised average is the mean, median, or mode? Why? _____

_____

7. If you were the toy company, which average would you advertise to entice more people into the store? _____

_____

8. Each of these sets of data below has an average of $30. If you are a comparison shopper, which store would you shop at? Why? _____

_____

Store A				
35	0	60	50	45
30	40	80	30	30

Store B				
10	30	28	22	38
50	15	45	15	47

Store C				
28	33	40	45	80
27	25	28	28	70

Brain Teaser 13 ꙮ ꙮ ꙮ ꙮ ꙮ ꙮ ꙮ ꙮ ꙮ ꙮ ꙮ ꙮ

Mind Your Numbers #1

Find the values for each set of letters.

1. Values: 1, 2, 3, 4

$a \times b = 8$

$a \times c = 2$

$a \times d = 6$

a = _____

b = _____

c = _____

d = _____

5. Values: 1, 2, 3, 8

$q \times r = 8$

$q \times s = 16$

$q \times t = 24$

q = _____

r = _____

s = _____

t = _____

9. Values: 2, 3, 4, 8

$i \times j = 6$

$i \times k = 8$

$i \times l = 16$

i = _____

j = _____

k = _____

l = _____

2. Values: 1, 4, 6, 10

$e \times f = 40$

$e \times g = 24$

$e \times h = 4$

e = _____

f = _____

g = _____

h = _____

6. Values: 1, 3, 6, 7

$u \times v = 18$

$u \times w = 42$

$u \times y = 6$

u = _____

v = _____

w = _____

y = _____

10. Values: 1, 6, 18, 19

$a \times b = 6$

$a \times c = 18$

$a \times d = 19$

a = _____

b = _____

c = _____

d = _____

3. Values: 1, 3, 6, 9

$i \times j = 6$

$i \times k = 54$

$i \times l = 18$

i = _____

j = _____

k = _____

l = _____

7. Values: 2, 3, 4, 10

$a \times b = 40$

$a \times c = 12$

$a \times d = 8$

a = _____

b = _____

c = _____

d = _____

11. Values: 4, 7, 15, 17

$e \times f = 105$

$e \times g = 60$

$e \times h = 255$

e = _____

f = _____

g = _____

h = _____

4. Values: 1, 3, 7, 9

$m \times n = 3$

$m \times o = 9$

$m \times p = 7$

m = _____

n = _____

o = _____

p = _____

8. Values: 5, 6, 7, 9

$e \times f = 42$

$e \times g = 35$

$e \times h = 63$

e = _____

f = _____

g = _____

h = _____

12. Values: 6, 10, 16, 17

$i \times j = 170$

$i \times k = 102$

$i \times l = 272$

i = _____

j = _____

k = _____

l = _____

Brain Teaser 14 ⟳ ⟳ ⟳ ⟳ ⟳ ⟳ ⟳ ⟳ ⟳ ⟳ ⟳ ⟳

Mind Your Numbers #2

Find the values for each set of letters.

1. Values: 12, 14, 16, 19

m x n = 228

m x o = 304

m x p = 266

m = _____

n = _____

o = _____

p = _____

2. Values: 17, 21, 24, 36

q x r = 408

q x s = 612

q x t = 357

q = _____

r = _____

s = _____

t = _____

3. Values: 16, 19, 72, 96

u x v = 6,912

u x w = 1,536

u x y = 1,824

u = _____

v = _____

w = _____

y = _____

4. Values: 11, 24, 45, 82

a x b = 1,968

a x c = 902

a x d = 3,690

a = _____

b = _____

c = _____

d = _____

5. Values: 19, 33, 47, 95

e x f = 3,135

e x g = 627

e x h = 1,551

e = _____

f = _____

g = _____

h = _____

6. Values: 10, 12, 13, 95

i x j = 1,235

i x k = 950

i x l = 1,140

i = _____

j = _____

k = _____

l = _____

7. Values: 1, 4, 9, 10

a x b = 4

b x c = 9

c x d = 90

a = _____

b = _____

c = _____

d = _____

8. Values: 1, 2, 5, 9

e x f = 45

f x g = 18

g x h = 2

e = _____

f = _____

g = _____

h = _____

9. Values: 2, 8, 9, 10

i x k – 16

j x l = 90

k x l = 18

i = _____

j = _____

k = _____

l = _____

10. Values: 1, 2, 6, 7

m x p = 42

o x n = 2

p x n = 6

m = _____

n = _____

o = _____

p = _____

11. Values: 2, 5, 6, 7

q x t = 14

r x s = 30

q x r = 42

q = _____

r = _____

s = _____

t = _____

12. Values: 2, 8, 9, 10

u x w = 90

v x y = 16

w x v = 20

u = _____

v = _____

w = _____

y = _____

Brain Teaser 15 ⟳ ⟳ ⟳ ⟳ ⟳ ⟳ ⟳ ⟳ ⟳ ⟳ ⟳ ⟳

Mind Your Numbers #3

Find the values for each set of letters.

1. Values: 1 6, 8, 10

$a \times d = 8$

$b \times c = 60$

$b \times d = 6$

a = _____

b = _____

c = _____

d = _____

5. Values: 1, 3, 5, 15

$15 \div h = f$

$15 \div f = 15$

$15 \div e = 3$

$15 \div g = 5$

e = _____

f = _____

g = _____

h = _____

9. Values: 3, 6, 8, 16

$48 \div x = 8$

$48 \div v = 16$

$48 \div w = v$

$48 \div u = x$

u = _____

v = _____

w = _____

x = _____

2. Values: 1, 3, 5, 8

$e \times g = 24$

$f \times h = 5$

$h \times g = 3$

e = _____

f = _____

g = _____

h = _____

6. Values: 2, 4, 5, 10

$20 \div j = 5$

$20 \div l = i$

$20 \div k = j$

$20 \div 10 = l$

i = _____

j = _____

k = _____

l = _____

10. Values: 4, 10, 10, 25

$100 \div c = a$

$100 \div 10 = c, a$

$100 \div 4 = b$

$100 \div d = b$

a = _____

b = _____

c = _____

d = _____

3. Values: 2, 4, 6, 8

$i \times l = 8$

$j \times k = 48$

$l \times j = 24$

i = _____

j = _____

k = _____

l = _____

7. Values: 3, 4, 6, 8

$24 \div 6 = p$

$24 \div m = 3$

$24 \div p = o$

$24 \div n = m$

m = _____

n = _____

o = _____

p = _____

11. Values: 20, 30, 40, 60

$120 \div f = 3$

$120 \div 2 = e$

$120 \div 6 = g$

$120 \div h = 4$

e = _____

f = _____

g = _____

h = _____

4. Values: 2, 3, 4, 6

$12 \div a = b$

$12 \div b = 4$

$12 \div c = d$

$12 \div d = 6$

a = _____

b = _____

c = _____

d = _____

8. Values: 3, 5, 6, 10

$30 \div r = 6$

$30 \div t = 3$

$30 \div q = t$

$30 \div s = r$

q = _____

r = _____

s = _____

t = _____

12. Values: 8, 10, 20, 25

$200 \div l = 8$

$200 \div j = 10$

$200 \div k = l$

$200 \div i = j$

i = _____

j = _____

k = _____

l = _____

Brain Teaser 16

After School Hours

Read each clue. If the answer is "yes," make an "O" in the box. If the answer is "no," make an "X" in the box.

	Monday	Tuesday	Wednesday	Thursday	Art Exhibit	Fair	Movie Premiere	Sporting Event
Ana								
Dave								
Mario								
Steve								

Clues

1. Ana went to her event earlier in the week than Steve.

2. Mario went to the sporting event but not on Monday.

3. Dave went to the premiere of *Attack of the Bugs* on Tuesday.

4. Steve went to the new art exhibit on Wednesday.

 Ana went to the _____ on _____.

 Dave went to the _____ on _____.

 Mario went to the _____ on _____.

 Steve went to the _____ on _____.

Brain Teaser 17 ⟋ ⟋ ⟋ ⟋ ⟋ ⟋ ⟋ ⟋ ⟋ ⟋ ⟋

Potluck Dinner

Read each clue. If the answer is "yes," make an "O" in the box. If the answer is "no" make an "X" in the box.

The Potluck Dinner Club is held every Friday night at 6:30. Read the clues to find the time each member arrived as well as the food item he/she brought.

	5:45	6:00	6:15	6:30	6:45	Dessert	Rolls	Salad	Sodas	Spaghetti
Betty										
Chaz										
Heidi										
Paul										
Roland										

Clues

1. Roland was late for the Potluck Dinner.

2. Betty arrived after Chaz.

3. Paul arrived before the person who brought the spaghetti.

4. Chaz's rolls were still warm when he arrived.

5. Heidi arrived right on time.

6. Paul didn't bring the salad or the soda.

7. Betty brought the spaghetti and Heidi brought the salad.

8. Betty arrived at 6:15 and Paul arrived before Chaz.

Betty arrived at _____ and brought the _____.

Chaz arrived at _____ and brought the _____.

Heidi arrived at _____ and brought the _____.

Paul arrived at _____ and brought the _____.

Roland arrived at _____ and brought the _____.

Brain Teaser 18

Doubling Money

1. At the start of each week, Maureen receives a dollar. Each day the amount of money Maureen receives doubles compared to the previous day. How much money total will Maureen have at the end of the week?

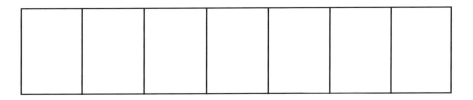

At the end of the week Maureen has been paid a total of _____.

---

2. John is paid every 10 days. The first day, John receives $5.00. Each day for the rest of the pay period, John's pay is doubled compared to the previous day. What is the amount of John's paycheck?

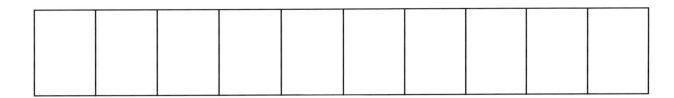

John's paycheck will be _____.

---

3. Henry is paid ten dollars the first day of the week. On each of the following days, his pay is doubled. How many days will it take him to earn at least a thousand dollars?

It will take Henry at least _____ days to earn a dollar a day.

Brain Teaser 19

Big Money

Denominations in Circulation

These are the coins and bills in general circulation in the United States today and the portrait on each coin or bill.

Denomination	Name	Portrait
$0.01	penny	Abraham Lincoln
$0.05	nickel	Thomas Jefferson
$0.10	dime	Franklin D. Roosevelt
$0.25	quarter	George Washington
$0.50	half-dollar	John F. Kennedy
$1.00	silver dollar	Dwight D. Eisenhower
$1.00	coin dollar	Susan B. Anthony
$1.00	dollar bill	George Washington
$2.00	2 dollar bill	Thomas Jefferson
$5.00	5 dollar bill	Abraham Lincoln
$10.00	10 dollar bill	Alexander Hamilton
$20.00	20 dollar bill	Andrew Jackson
$50.00	50 dollar bill	Ulysses S. Grant
$100.00	100 dollar bill	Benjamin Franklin
$500.00	500 dollar bill	William McKinley
$1,000.00	1,000 dollar bill	Grover Cleveland
$5,000.00	5,000 dollar bill	James Madison
$10,000.00	10,000 dollar bill	Salmon P. Chase

The United States government no longer produces currency larger than $100 dollar bills.

Currency in Circulation

This chart lists the currency in circulation by denomination in 1998. The numbers are rounded off to the nearest tenth of a billion dollars.

Currency in Circulation (1998)

Coins	$ 25.1 billion
$1.00	$ 6.4 billion
$2.00	$ 1.1 billion
$5.00	$ 7.4 billion
$10.00	$ 1.33 billion
$20.00	$ 82.7 billion
$50.00	$ 46.7 billion
$100.00	$292.6 billion
$500.00	$ .1 billion
$1,000.00	$ .2 billion

The total currency in the United States in 1998 was $463.6 billion dollars.

Brain Teaser 19 *(cont.)* ୬ ୯ ୯ ୬ ୯ ୬ ୯ ୬ ୬ ୯

Big Money *(cont.)*

Directions: Use the charts on the previous page and a calculator to help you answer these questions.

1. If you had exactly one coin and one bill of every denomination of United States currency listed on the chart, how much money would that be worth?

   Answer: $_____

2. How many hundred dollar bills would it take to equal a thousand dollar bill?

   Answer: _____

3. How many ten dollar bills would it take to equal a five hundred dollar bill?

   Answer: _____

4. How many five dollar bills would it take to equal a five thousand dollar bill?

   Answer: _____

5. How many quarters would it take to equal a ten dollar bill?

   Answer: _____

6. How many quarters would it take to equal a one hundred dollar bill?

   Answer: _____

7. There are $1.1 billion dollars worth of two dollar bills in circulation. How many two dollar bills are actually in circulation?

   Answer: _____

8. There are about $7,400,000,000 worth of five dollar bills in circulation. How many actual five dollar bills would that equal?

   Answer: _____

9. How many quarters would it take to equal one ten thousand dollar bill?

   Answer: _____

Brain Teaser 20 ⟡ ⟡ ⟡ ⟡ ⟡ ⟡ ⟡ ⟡ ⟡ ⟡ ⟡

Working with Charts and Graphs

This graph illustrates the amount of revenue (taxes) collected by nine states in 1996. The amounts indicated are rounded to the nearest billion dollars.

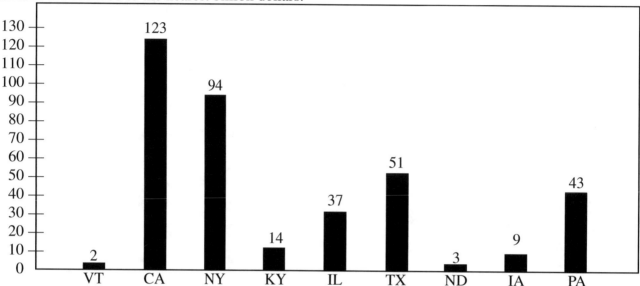

Directions: Use the graph to answer these questions.

1. Which state collected the most money in 1996? _____

2. Which two states collected the least money in 1996?

   _____   _____

3. Which three states collected as much money together as Kentucky did alone?

   _____   _____   _____

4. How much more money did California collect than Illinois?

   _____

5. Which two states together collected as much money as New York did alone?

   _____   _____

6. What was the total revenue collected by all nine states? _____

The total revenue collected by the 50 United States was about 967 billion dollars. (Percentage can be calculated by dividing the whole into a part.)

7. What percentage of the total was collected by New York? _____

8. What percentage of the total was collected by California? _____

9. What percentage of the total was collected by Vermont? _____

Brain Teaser 21 ⟩ ❧ ⟩ ❧ ⟩ ❧ ⟩ ❧ ⟩ ⟩ ❧

Working with Circle Graphs

This circle graph illustrates the national percentage of personal consumption (spending), rounded to the nearest percent for 10 separate categories in 1997.

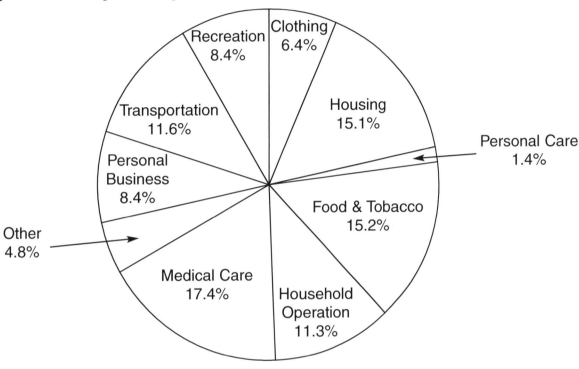

Directions: Use the circle graph to answer these questions.

1. Which two categories represent the same percentage of spending?

   _____   _____

2. Which item takes up the largest percentage of personal spending in the United States?

   _____

3. Personal care includes items such as toothpaste, hair care products, and makeup. What percentage of personal spending is spent on personal care products? _____

4. Which two items have an almost identical amount of spending?

   _____   _____

5. What is the total percentage of spending used for housing and household operation, such as cleaning, phones, water, and so forth?

   _____

Directions: Personal consumption expenditures in 1997 totaled 5.4937 trillion dollars. Use the percentages on the circle graph and this number to answer these questions. Use a calculator. Round your answer to the nearest hundredth.

6. How many dollars were spent on housing in 1997? _____

7. How many dollars were spent on food and tobacco in 1997? _____

8. How many dollars were spent on medical care in 1997? _____

9. How many dollars were spent on transportation in 1997? _____

Brain Teaser 22 ꕥ ꔀ ꕥ ꔀ ꕥ ꔀ ꕥ ꔀ ꕥ ꔀ ꕥ ꔀ

Fancy Factorials

Directions: Place four crayons—one red, one blue, one green, and one yellow—on your desk. Find out how many different ways you can arrange them. Complete the chart below.

red	blue	green	yellow
red	blue	yellow	green
red	green	blue	yellow
red	green	yellow	blue
red	yellow	green	blue
red	yellow	blue	green
blue	red	green	yellow
blue	red	yellow	green
blue	green	red	yellow
blue	green	yellow	red
blue	yellow	green	red
blue	yellow	red	green
green	blue	red	yellow
green	blue	yellow	_____
green	red	_____	_____
green	_____	_____	_____
_____	_____	_____	_____
_____	_____	_____	_____
yellow	_____	_____	_____
_____	_____	_____	_____
_____	_____	_____	_____
_____	_____	_____	_____
_____	_____	_____	_____

Directions: Use a factorial to help you answer these questions.

1. You received three trophies: one for soccer, one for baseball, and one for track. How many different ways could you arrange these three trophies on your dresser? _____

2. You have four coins: one dime, one nickel, one penny, and one quarter. How many different ways can you arrange them in order on your desk? _____

3. You have a pencil and a pen. How many different ways can you arrange them in order in your shirt pocket? _____

Brain Teaser 23 ೨ ☙ ೨ ☙ ೨ ☙ ೨ ☙ ೨ ☙ ೨ ೨ ☙

More Fancy Factorials

Directions: Place five crayons—one red, one blue, one green, one yellow, and one orange—on your desk. Find out how many different ways you can arrange them. Fill in the blanks on this chart. (*Note:* R = red, B = blue, G = green, Y = yellow, and O = orange)

R	B	G	Y	O
R	B	G	O	Y
R	B	Y	O	G
R	B	Y	G	O
R	B	O	Y	G
R	B	O	G	Y
R	G	B	Y	O
R	G	B	O	Y
R	G	Y	O	B
R	G	Y	B	O
R	G	O	Y	B
R	G	O	B	Y
R	Y	G	B	O
R	Y	G	O	B
R	___	___	___	___
R	___	___	___	___
R	___	___	___	___
R	___	___	___	___
R	O	___	___	___
R	O	___	___	___
R	___	___	___	___
R	___	___	___	___
R	___	___	___	___
R	___	___	___	___

1. This chart shows only the arrangements with red as the first color. How many different arrangements could you create for all five colors?

    $$5! = 5 \times 4 \times 3 \times 2 \times 1 =$$

2. Write a factorial to indicate how many ways six crayons could be arranged. Then compute the numerical value of 6!.

3. Write a factorial to indicate how many ways seven crayons could be arranged.

Brain Teaser 24 ॰ ☺ ॰ ॰ ☺ ॰ ☺ ॰ ☺ ॰ ☺ ॰ ॰ ☺

Cute Combinations

Directions: Solve these problems using combinations. Make a chart and check the answer with multiplication. The first one is started for you.

1. You have 4 T-shirts (white, green, blue, and yellow) and 3 pairs of jeans (brown, black, and purple). How many combinations can you wear? 4 x 3 = _____

Combinations Chart

white T-shirt with brown jeans   white T-shirt with black jeans

white T-shirt with purple jeans   green T-shirt with brown jeans

_____   _____

_____   _____

_____   _____

_____   _____

---

2. You have 6 T-shirts (white, blue, green, yellow, red, and pink) and 2 pairs of jeans (black and brown). How many combinations can you wear? _____ x _____ = _____

Combinations Chart

Directions: Use multiplication to do these problems.

3. You have 9 shirts and 6 pairs of jeans. How many combinations can you wear?
   _____ x _____ = _____

4. You have 11 shirts and 12 pairs of pants. How many combinations can you wear?
   _____ x _____ = _____

5. You have 2 hats, 4 shirts, and 3 jeans. How many combinations can you wear?
   _____ x _____ x _____ = _____

6. You have 2 hats, 5 shirts, 4 jeans, and 2 pairs of shoes. How many combinations can you wear?
   _____ x _____ x _____ x _____ = _____

Brain Teaser 25 ꙮ ꙮ ꙮ ꙮ ꙮ ꙮ ꙮ ꙮ ꙮ ꙮ ꙮ ꙮ

Simple Permutations

Directions: Use factorials to solve these permutations. (*Remember:* The order matters with permutations. AB is different from BA.)

1. You have 3 books to stack in as many different arrangements as you can.

    3! = 3 x 2 x 1 = _____

2. You have 4 trophies to arrange in as many different arrangements as you can.

    4! = _____ x _____ x _____ x _____ = _____

3. You have 5 baseball cards to organize in as many different arrangements as you can.

    _____! = _____ x _____ x _____ x _____ x _____ = _____

4. You have 6 coats to hang in the closet in as many different arrangements as you can.

    _____! = _____ x _____ x _____ x _____ x _____ x _____ = _____

Directions: Determine the number of permutations or possible arrangements for each of these problems. Each problem is started for you.

5. You have 4 books altogether and must arrange these books 3 at a time.

    Step 1: Subtract the number of books used at one time from the total number.
    $$4 - 3 = 1$$
    Step 2: Write the factorial used to express the arrangement.
    4!/1!   (4 factorial divided by 1 factorial)
    Step 3: Solve the problem. $\dfrac{4 \times 3 \times 2 \times 1}{1}$

    Step 4: The answer is 4 x 3 x 2 or _____.

6. You have 7 books altogether and must arrange these books 3 at a time.

    Step 1: Subtract the number of books used at one time from the total number.
    $$7 - 3 = 4$$
    Step 2: Write the factorial used to express the arrangement.
    7!/4!   (7 factorial divided by 4 factorial)
    Step 3: Solve the problem.
    $$\dfrac{7 \times 6 \times 5 \times 4 \times 3 \times 2 \times 1}{4 \times 3 \times 2 \times 1}$$
    Step 4: The answer is 7 x 6 x 5 or _____.

7. You have 9 books altogether and must arrange these books 4 at a time.

    Step 1: Subtract the number of books used at one time from the total number.
    $$9 - 4 = _____$$
    Step 2: Write the factorial used to express the arrangement.
    9!/5!   (9 factorial divided by 5 factorial)
    Step 3: Solve the problem.
    Step 4: The answer is 9 x 8 x 7 x 6 or _____.

Brain Teaser 26 ⟳ ◎ ⟳ ⟳ ◎ ⟳ ◎ ⟳ ⟳ ◎ ⟳ ⟳ ◎

Challenging Word Problems

Solve each word problem.

1. Pam and Jane are sisters. Pam is twice as old as Jane. Together their combined age is 24. How old are Pam and Jane?

   Pam is _____ years old.   Jane is _____ years old.

2. The Sanford brothers are all separated by the same number of years. When added together, their combined age is 30. Maurice is three times older than the youngest brother. Ray is twice as old as the youngest brother, Mark. How old is each brother?

   Maurice is _____ years old.   Ray is _____ years old.

   Mark is _____ years old.

3. The four Nightingale kids range in age from 1 to 8. The sum of their ages is 15. Jerry is twice as old as Fran. Brent is twice as old as Jerry. Charlotte is twice as old as Brent. How old is each one of the Nightingale kids?

   Jerry is_____ years old.   Brent is _____ years old.

   Fran is _____ years old.   Charlotte is _____ years old.

4. Steven Baxter is three times older than Keith. Bryan is ⅓ younger than Steven. How old are Bryan, Keith, and Steven?

   Steven is _____ years old.   Keith is _____ years old.

   Bryan is_____ years old.

5. Juanita is ½ the age of her mother. Juanita's younger sister Benita is ¼ her mother's age. If their mother is 56, how old are Juanita and Benita?

   Juanita is _____ years old.   Benita is _____ years old.

6. The Martinez family has three children. Raphael is 5 years older than his brother Miguel. Miguel is 8 years younger than his sister Maria. If Maria is the oldest and Miguel is 7 years old, how old are Maria and Raphael?

   Maria is _____ years old.   Raphael is _____ years old.

7. Noriko's grandmother celebrated her 79th birthday in 2003 and her grandfather celebrated his 83rd birthday during the same year. In what year was each grandparent born?

   Noriko's grandmother _____   Noriko's grandfather _____

8. Patrick and Holden are cousins and are the same age. Patrick just celebrated his 15th birthday on June 27, 2003. During the same year, Holden's birthday will be celebrated on September 17th. How many days apart were Patrick and Holden born?

   Patrick and Holden were born _____ days apart.

Brain Teaser 27 ᕙ ❤ ᕗ ᕙ ❤ ᕗ ᕙ ❤ ᕗ ᕙ ❤ ᕗ ᕙ ᕗ ❤

More Challenging Word Problems

Directions: Use some of the different methods you've learned to solve word problems in tackling these brain teasers.

Frog Race

Frog 1 and frog 2 have a race. Frog 1 makes a jump of 80 centimeters once every 5 seconds. Frog 2 makes a jump of 15 centimeters every 1 second. The rules of the race state that the frogs must cross a line 5 meters away and then return to the starting point. Which frog wins the race? _____

Bad Dogs!

Three neighborhood dogs barked all last night. Lolly, Patches, and Lady began barking together at 11:00 p.m. Then, Lolly barked every 5 minutes, Patches barked every 8 minutes, and Lady barked every 12 minutes. Later that night, Mrs. Mikes awakened when all three dogs barked together again. What time did Mrs. Mikes wake up? _____

Free Dinner

At the Heartland Cafe, you get a free dinner after every 8 dinners you buy. If you ate there 45 times last year, how many of those dinners were free? _____

Race to Rescue

A child in a mountain village has fallen ill. Benjamin, his brother Joshua, and his sister Hannah must get their father, the village doctor, who is gathering herbs on the other side of the mountain. To make sure they get to him as quickly as possible, they decide to split up.

> Joshua will ride his horse around the mountain's base.
> Benjamin will travel by river raft.
> Hannah will climb the steep cliff trail.

- The raft can travel at 22 miles an hour along the 40 miles of the river, but there are 3 places where Benjamin, at each place, will lose 0.4 hours by having to carry the raft past waterfalls.

- Joshua's horse can travel 15 miles per hour on the flatter part of the 32-mile trail but only 8 miles per hour on the steep part, which is 30% of the whole trail.

- Hannah's road up and down the cliffs is the shortest, only 14 miles, but her average rate is only 5 miles an hour, and she must take a 10-minute rest at the top of the trail.

Provided Benjamin does not hit a rock, Joshua is not attacked by wild animals, and Hannah is not bitten by a snake, who will reach their father first? (Round all decimals to tenths.) _____

Brain Teaser 28 ◑ ◉ ◑ ◉ ◑ ◉ ◑ ◉ ◑ ◑ ◉

Tricky Word Problems

Clever Math Teachers

Math teachers just love playing math games. At Median Middle School, for example, the math teachers put signs on their doors to say whether they are at school or not. What they do is each post a true or untrue number sentence on the door. The teachers who are at school post problems with true answers. Here is what they posted last Tuesday.

Mr. Perry Meter:	$4 \times 12 = 12 + 12 + 12 + 12 + 12$
Mr. Ric Tangle:	$32{,}768 \times 12{,}597 = 12{,}597 \times 32{,}768$
Ms. Py R. Square:	$50 \times 32 > 1{,}000$
Mr. Sol Ution:	$1/4 + 1/4 = 1/8$
Ms. Dee Nominator:	$572 \times 43{,}176 = 572 \times 43{,}196$
Mr. Cal Culator:	$33 + z = 107; z = 64$

Who is in school? _____

_____

_____

Who is not in school? _____

_____

_____

At the Corner Store

Dave went into a corner store. He purchased four items.

"That will be $7.11," said the cashier.

"Wow!" Dave said. "How did you get $7.11?"

"Oh, I just multiplied the four items."

"What?! You're supposed to add the prices of the items, not multiply them."

"Makes no difference," said the cashier. "Comes out the same."

What were the prices of the four items?

Hint: *Three are under $2.00.*

Time Activity

Think how the day can be broken up into 24 hours. The time spent sleeping, eating, going to school, etc., can be expressed as fractional parts of the day. In this activity, 24 will be used as the denominator in all of the fractions. If you sleep 8 hours, then the fractional part of the day spent sleeping is 8/24. Use hours, not minutes. Show how you spend your 24-hour day as a chart. Make a fraction for each activity category in the day. Your activities total 24/24.

Brain Teaser 29

More Tricky Word Problems

Bare Feet

There are 12 people in a room. 6 people are wearing socks, 4 people are wearing shoes, and 3 people are wearing both. How many people are in bare feet? _____

Two Trains Running (Everyone's Favorite)

A freight train leaves a station at 4:00 p.m. traveling at 30 kilometers per hour. A passenger train leaves 1 hour later, traveling at 50 kilometers per hour. At what time will the passenger train overtake the freight train? _____

Hint: Look at the problem as "starting" when both trains have started moving.

Sheep or Kids?

This problem has more than one answer. Long ago, villagers were building a bridge. While working under the bridge, Rodney could see only the legs of those walking by. He counted 10 legs in one group. What combination of sheep and children could have been in that group?

_____

Hint: Guess and check different combinations.

The Airplane and the Square

An airplane flies around a square which has sides 100 miles long. It takes the first side at 100 mph, the second side at 200 mph, the third side at 300 mph, and the fourth side at 400 mph.

What is the average speed of the plane in its flight around the square? _____

Hint: This is another time/distance/rate problem. You need to find out how long it took the airplane to travel each side for a total travel time.

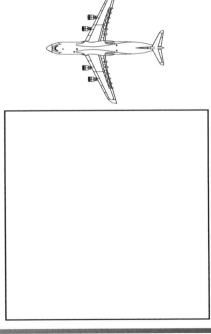

Brain Teaser 30 ᗧ ☻ ᗧ ☻ ᗧ ☻ ᗧ ☻ ᗧ ᗧ ☻

Computing Rate of Speed, Distance, or Time

How fast is a bicycle traveling if it covers 25 miles in 5 hours?

   Rate = Distance divided by Time or $R = \dfrac{D}{T}$ $R = \dfrac{25}{5}$ $R = 5$ miles per hour (m.p.h.)

Directions: Solve these problems. The first one is started for you. (*Remember:* Rate is how fast something is traveling.)

1. Your principal rode a bicycle 100 miles in 20 hours. What was his rate of speed in miles per hour? _____

2. The fifth-grade teacher drove a truck 200 miles through the snow in 8 hours. What was the teacher's average speed? _____

3. Your basketball coach rode his bicycle 77 miles in 14 hours. What was his average rate of speed? _____

4. The soccer coach ran 26.1 miles in 3 hours. What was his average speed? _____

5. The Boy Scouts leader hiked a trail that was 96 miles long in 40 hours. What was his average speed? _____

How far did a car travel which was moving at 35 miles per hour for 5 hours?

   Distance = Rate of Speed multiplied by the Time or $D = RT$

   $D = 35 \times 5 = D = 175$ miles

6. The football coach drove his truck at 50 miles per hour for 5 hours. How far did he drive? _____

7. The third-grade teacher flew a plane at 120 miles per hour for 7 hours. How far did the teacher travel? _____

8. The kindergarten teacher hiked along a trail for 9 hours at 1.25 miles per hour. How far did she walk? _____

9. A stock car traveled at 195 miles per hour for 3 hours. How far did it travel? _____

10. A cross-country runner traveled for 7 hours at 5.3 miles per hour. How far did the runner go? _____

How long did a boy run who ran 30 miles at the rate of 6 miles per hour?

   Time = Distance divided by Rate of Speed or $T = \dfrac{D}{R}$

   $T = \dfrac{30}{6}$ $T = 5$ hours

11. Your teacher drove 1,500 miles from San Diego to Seattle at 50 miles per hour. How many hours did she drive? _____

12. You rode a dirt bike 42 miles through some rough canyons at 14 miles per hour. How many hours did you ride the bike? _____

13. The first-grade teacher rode a motorcycle 420 miles from Los Angeles to Phoenix at a rate of 40 miles per hour. How many hours did he ride? _____

14. The sixth-grade teacher drove 3,250 miles from Los Angeles to Washington, D.C., at the rate of 50 miles per hour. How many hours did the teacher drive? _____

15. Your best friend rode a bike 44 miles through the streets of your city at an average speed of 5.5 miles per hour. How many hours did your friend ride? _____

Brain Teaser 31

Apartment Living

Find each person's apartment.

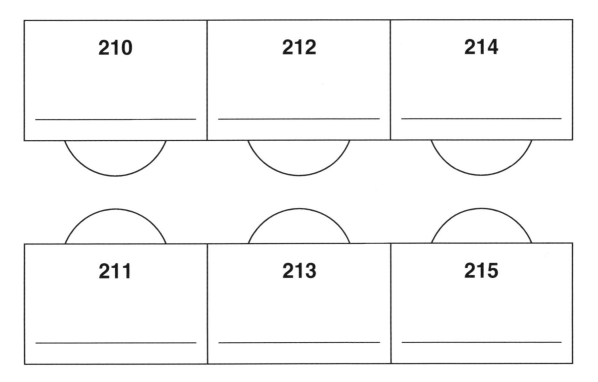

210	212	214

211	213	215

1. Brandon lives directly across from Adam and in between Violet and Maria.

2. Gary lives directly across from Violet and next door to a boy.

3. Maria lives directly across from another girl.

4. Brandon lives in an odd numbered apartment.

5. Maria lives in apartment number 215.

 Adam lives in apartment number

_____.

 Louisa lives in apartment number

_____.

 Brandon lives in apartment number

_____.

 Maria lives in apartment number

_____.

 Gary lives in apartment number

_____.

 Violet lives in apartment number

_____.

Brain Teaser 32

Family Dinner

Use the clues below to find each family member's place at the dinner table.

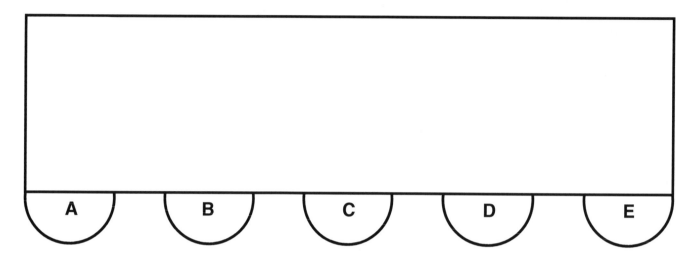

Clues

1. Adam sits in between Gary and Louisa.

2. Maria sits to the left of Louisa.

3. Brandon sits two chairs to the right of Adam.

 Adam sits in chair _____.   Louisa sits in chair _____.

 Brandon sits in chair _____.   Maria sits in chair _____.

 Gary sits in chair _____.

Brain Teaser 33

A Mazeful of Prime Numbers

Find your way through the maze by coloring only the prime numbers.

Start

		30	164	148	128	105	135	117	156
141	151	148	100	112	5	71	97	53	134
164	29	123	114	129	89	158	121	101	147
155	67	106	122	43	109	111	165	7	126
47	139	9	150	113	116	142	104	179	152
3	115	143	130	1	163	99	41	73	102
107	98	159	96	88	127	84	179	120	140
103	144	96	13	163	37	80	229	199	161
59	124	13	163	38	80	160	132	167	110
137	92	131	138	81	160	132	87	157	94
11	157	17	90	154	86	125	119	173	133
145	118	91	166	85	146	77	85		

Finish

Brain Teaser 34

Polygons and Axioms

In order to solve geometric problems, some general principles are used. Axioms, at one time called "self-evident truths," are basic mathematical principles. There are several axioms with which you may already be familiar since you have probably performed mathematical operations using them. Think of a situation in which you used this axiom: "If equals are added to equals, the sums are equal."

Here is an axiom.

> **The whole is greater than any of its parts, and it is equal to the sum of all of its parts.**

Can you demonstrate that the whole is equal to the sum of its parts using the polygons below? Cut out the polygons and arrange them so that they form a square. Then, find the necessary areas to show that this axiom is correct. To help you get started, use the following information:

- The area of section D is 12 cm².
- The area of the whole (square) is 144 cm².

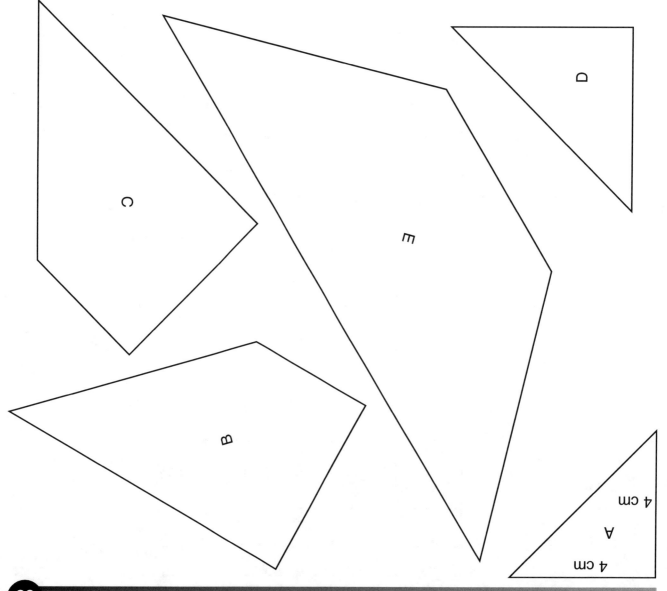

Brain Teaser 35

Multitude of Angles

Types of Angles

Each triangle has three angles. Angles have a vertex (point) and two sides (rays). Angles are measured by degrees. If one ray makes one whole revolution, it will sweep 360°.

A right angle measures 90°. Any angle less than a right angle is an acute angle. Any angle greater than a right angle and less than a straight angle is called an obtuse angle. Now you have four angles you can refer to: *acute, right, obtuse,* and *straight.* (The other angle which is not often used is a *reflex* angle. This is an angle that is more than 180°.)

On a separate sheet of paper, find and name (acute, right, obtuse, straight, or reflex) all the angles in this figure. Make a chart showing all the angles you found and label each angle with its correct name.

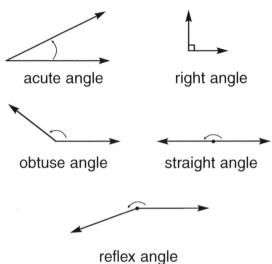

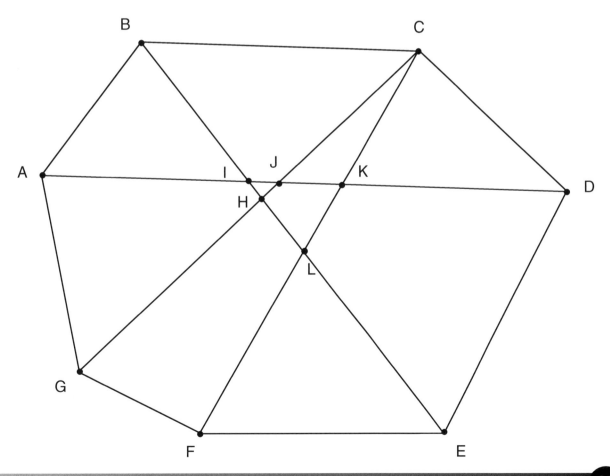

Brain Teaser 36 ᗡ ᒼ ᗡ ᒼ ᗡ ᒼ ᒼ ᗡ ᒼ ᗡ ᗡ ᒼ

Super Sets

Sets

A *set* is a well-defined collection of objects.

- A set may be defined by listing all of the objects in the set.

  Set A = {a, e, i, o, u}

- A set may be defined by naming a rule which determines exactly whether a given object belongs in the set.

  Set B = {all of the consonants in English}

Universal Set

The *universal set* is the set containing all of the objects of concern in a given problem. U is the symbol for the universal set. A universal set could include the following:

- all of the presidents of the United States
- the counting numbers from 1 through 20
- all even numbers up to 100
- all of the cities in California

Empty Set

The *empty set* is a set that contains no elements. The empty set is also called the *null set*. This is the symbol for the empty set: ∅. Look at the examples below.

- The set of all cities on Mars is an empty set.
- The set of all people weighing over 3,000 pounds is an empty set.
- The set of all odd numbers divisible by 2 is an empty set.

Subset

A *subset* is a set which contains part or all of the elements of another set. For example, {$a, e, i, o,$ u} is a subset of letters.

Union of Sets

The *union* of two or more sets is the combination of all of the elements of the original sets into one set. No member is left out, and no member is repeated. This is the symbol for union: ∪. Study the example.

  The set of all prime numbers under 10 = {2, 3, 5, 7}.
  The set of all odd numbers under 10 = {1, 3, 5, 7, 9}.
  The union of the two sets is {1, 2, 3, 5, 7, 9}.

Intersection of Sets

The *intersection* of two or more sets contains only those elements common to and found within each of the original sets. This is the symbol for intersection: ∩. Look at the example below.

  Set A = {1, 3, 5, 7, 9}

  Set B = {2, 3, 5, 7}

  The intersection of sets A and B is {3, 5, 7}.

Brain Teaser 36 *(cont.)* ᕫ ᕫ ᕫ ᕫ ᕫ ᕫ ᕫ ᕫ ᕫ ᕫ

Super Sets *(cont.)*

Directions: List the elements of the union of each trio of sets listed below. List the intersections indicated in each problem.

1. Set A = {1, 2, 3, 4, 5, 6}
   Set B = {1, 2, 4, 6, 8, 10}
   Set C = {1, 2, 3, 5, 9, 11}
   a. union of A, B, and C = {_____}
   b. intersection of A and B = {_____}
   c. intersection of B and C = {_____}
   d. intersection of A, B, and C = {_____}

2. Set D = {2, 3, 5, 7, 11}
   Set E = {1, 4, 9, 16, 25}
   Set F = {1, 3, 6, 10, 15, 21}
   a. union of D, E, and F = {_____}
   b. intersection of D and E = {_____}
   c. intersection of E and F = {_____}
   d. intersection of D, E, and F = {_____}

3. Set G = {3, 6, 9, 12, 15}
   Set H = {2, 4, 6, 8, 10, 12, 14}
   Set I = {4, 8, 12, 16}
   a. union of G, H, and I = {_____}
   b. intersection of G and H = {_____}
   c. intersection of H and I = {_____}
   d. intersection of G, H, and I = {_____}

4. Set J = {6, 12, 18, 24, 30, 36}
   Set K = {8, 16, 24, 32, 40}
   Set L = {4, 8, 12, 16, 20, 24, 28, 32, 36, 40}
   a. union of J, K, and L = {_____}
   b. intersection of J and K = {_____}
   c. intersection of K and L = {_____}
   d. intersection of J, K, and L = {_____}

Directions: Create your own sets. Determine the union and intersections.

5. Set P = {_____}
   Set Q = {_____}
   Set R = {_____}
   a. union of P, Q, and R = {_____}
   b. intersection of P and Q = {_____}
   c. intersection of Q and R = {_____}
   d. intersection of P, Q, and R = {_____}

Brain Teaser 37 ✺ ✺ ✺ ✺ ✺ ✺ ✺ ✺ ✺ ✺ ✺ ✺

Venn Diagrams

A *Venn diagram* can be used to illustrate the relationships between sets and subsets within a universal set. The universal set is enclosed within a rectangle. The other sets and subsets are enclosed by circles or interlocking circles.

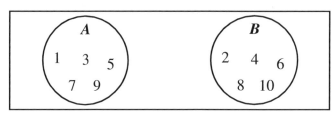

In the sample above, the universal set includes the counting numbers from 1 through 10. One circle encloses Set *A* which has the odd elements of the universal set. The second circle encloses Set *B* which has the even elements within the universal set.

Disjoint Sets

Disjoint sets have no elements in common. The sample above illustrates two disjoint sets. The two sets below are also disjoint. Set *C* has prime numbers. Set *D* has composite numbers.

Set *C* = {2, 3, 5, 7, 11}

Set *D* = {4, 6, 8, 9, 10}

Union of Sets with Venn Diagrams

This example shows the union of sets *E* and *F*. Both circles are shaded.

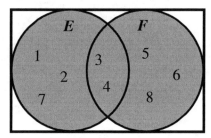

Set *E* = {1, 2, 3, 4, 7}

Set *F* = {3, 4, 5, 6, 8}

union of *E* and *F* = {1, 2, 3, 4, 5, 6, 7, 8}

Intersection of Sets with Venn Diagrams

This example shows the intersection of sets *E* and *F*. Only the overlapping part of the interlocked circle is shaded.

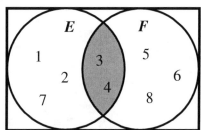

intersection of *E* and *F* = {3, 4}

Brain Teaser 37 (cont.)

Venn Diagrams (cont.)

Directions: List the elements in the union of each diagram shown here. List the elements in the intersection of each diagram shown here.

1.

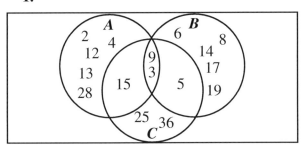

    a. Union of sets *A* and *B*:

    {_____}

    b. Union of sets *C* and *B*:

    {_____}

    c. Union of sets *A*, *B*, and *C*:

    {_____}

    d. Intersection of sets *A* and *B*:

    {_____}

    e. Intersection of sets *C* and *B*:

    {_____}

    f. Intersection of sets *A*, *B*, and *C*:

    {_____}

2.

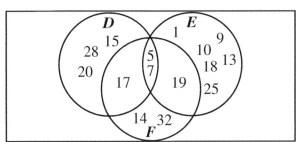

    a. Union of sets *D* and *E*:

    {_____}

    b. Union of sets *F* and *E*:

    {_____}

    c. Union of sets *D*, *E*, and *F*:

    {_____}

    d. Intersection of sets *D* and *E*:

    {_____}

    e. Intersection of sets *F* and *E*:

    {_____}

    f. Intersection of sets *D*, *E*, and *F*:

    {_____}

3.

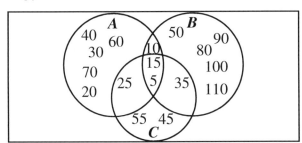

    a. Union of sets *A* and *B*:

    {_____}

    b. Union of sets *C* and *B*:

    {_____}

    c. Union of sets *A*, *B*, and *C*:

    {_____}

    d. Intersection of sets *A* and *B*:

    {_____}

    e. Intersection of sets *C* and *B*:

    {_____}

    f. Intersection of sets *A*, *B*, and *C*:

    {_____}

4.

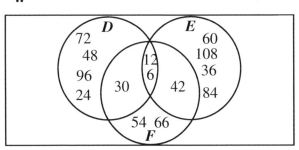

    a. Union of sets *D* and *F*:

    {_____}

    b. Union of sets *D* and *E*:

    {_____}

    c. Union of sets *D*, *E*, and *F*:

    {_____}

    d. Intersection of sets *D* and *F*:

    {_____}

    e. Intersection of sets *D* and *E*:

    {_____}

    f. Intersection of sets *D*, *E*, and *F*:

    {_____}

Brain Teaser 38 ◔ ◕ ◔ ◕ ◔ ◕ ◔ ◕ ◔ ◕ ◔ ◕

Solving for the Unknown #1

Directions: Use your knowledge of addition and subtraction to break these codes. Use a calculator if you have one.

1. 54 + 29 JA	**2.** 67 + 99 F I I	**3.** 145 + 366 BFF	**4.** 98 + FG 110
5. 87 + C J 165	**6.** 247 + ACD 626	**7.** HF + 76 117	**8.** BI + 99 155
9. DGA + 756 1679	**10.** CJ2 + 44B 1227	**11.** B82 + B11 1093	**12.** G9E + 245 535
13. FF + FF 22	**14.** AAA + AA 366	**15.** HHHH + HHHH 8888	**16.** 98 − 38 RM
17. 484 − 149 UUN	**18.** 976 − 286 RZM	**19.** 567 − WUX 333	**20.** 974 − PZQ 176
21. 765 − VNV 614	**22.** QWU − 134 689	**23.** PZMV − 1236 6665	**24.** ZWUX − 4265 4969
25. ZZZ − ZZ 9MM	**26.** VVVV − VV 11MM	**27.** PPZZ − PP 7722	**28.** XXXX − W00W W X 4 2
29. UVV − 30 281	**30.** RR0R − UU43 3263	**31.** WWWWWW − WWWW1 W00001	**32.** QQQQQ − XXX4X 4xx4x

Brain Teaser 39 ∂ ☙ ∂ ☙ ∂ ☙ ∂ ☙ ∂ ∂ ☙

Solving for the Unknown #2

Directions: Use your knowledge of multiplication to break these codes. Use a calculator if you have one.

1.
```
    45   S = _____
  x  S
   180
```
2.
```
    87   P = _____
  x  P
   174
```
3.
```
    39   Y = _____
  x  Y
   351
```
4.
```
    88   R = _____
  x  R
   440
```

5.
```
   136   C= _____
  x  C
   952
```
6.
```
   254   T= _____
  x  T
  2032
```
7.
```
    97   C= _____
  x  8   B = _____
   CCB
```
8.
```
   339   P = _____
  x  7   X = _____
  PXCX   C = _____
```

9.
```
   764   S = _____
  x  6   R = _____
  SRTS   T = _____
```
10.
```
    35   P = _____
  x PL   L = _____
   700
```
11.
```
    56   C = _____
  x CL   L = _____
  3920
```
12.
```
    98   B = _____
  x BL   L = _____
  5880
```

13.
```
     87   M = _____
  x  MM   T = _____
     87   C = _____
  + TC0
    957
```
14.
```
     62   R = _____
  x  RR   X = _____
    310   M = _____
  + XM00
   3410
```
15.
```
     74   C = _____
  x  CC   R = _____
    518   M = _____
  + RMT0  T = _____
   5698
```
16.
```
     AA   A = _____
  x  AA
     AA
  + AA0
    A2A
```

17.
```
    CCC   C = _____
  x  CC
   8CC1
  + 8CC10
  98C01
```
18.
```
    EEE   E = _____
  x  EE   C = _____
    CCC
  + CCC0
  10989
```
19.
```
    JED   J = _____
  x  32   E = _____
    870   D = _____
  + 13050 A = _____
  AECB0   C = _____
          B = _____
```
20.
```
    GCF   G = _____
  x  78   C = _____
   7168   F = _____
  + 62720
  FCGGG
```

21.
```
    KFG   K = _____
  x  29   F = _____
   6912   G = _____
  + 15360 B = _____
  BBBKB
```
22.
```
   FFGG   F = _____
  x   5   G = _____
  33440
```
23.
```
   ABCD   A = _____
  x  70   B = _____
  90650   C = _____
          D = _____
```
24.
```
   DJAF   D = _____
  x 400   J = _____
 2166400  A = _____
          F = _____
```

25. KKKK x K = 54,439   K = _____

26. DDDDD x DD = 3,055,525   D = _____

Answer Key

Page 4
1. $1 \times 9 \times 8 \div 12 = 6$
2. $15 \times 15 \div 5 \div 9 \times 3 = 15$
3. $56 \div 4 \div 7 \times 2 = 4$
4. $156 \div 4 \times 2 \times 2 = 156$
5. $635 \times 6 \div 10 \div 3 = 127$
6. $77 \div 11 \times 8 \div 14 = 4$
7. $25 \times 60 \div 10 \div 15 = 10$
8. $72 \div 8 \times 9 \times 4 \div 6 = 54$
9. $145 \div 5 \times 4 \times 2 = 232$
10. $8460 \div 10 \div 94 \times 2 = 18$

Page 5
1. $144 \div 12 = 12$
2. $616 \div 14 = 44$
3. $319 \div 29 = 11$
4. $375 \div 15 = 25$
5. $945 \div 15 = 63$
6. $2576 \div 46 = 56$
7. $3900 \div 260 = 15$
8. $1729 \div 91 = 19$
9. $4899 \div 71 = 69$
10. $5985 \div 399 = 15$

Page 6
1. 3
2. Fred is 18, and Paul is 16.
3. 16
4. 2
5. a quarter; 15 minutes

Page 7
James Madison

Page 8
1. 4
2. 2
3. 3
4. 4
5. 2
6. 5
7. 16
8. 60
9. 2
10. 1/2
11. .33 or 1/3
12. 2
13. .33 or 1/3
14. .4
15. 2
16. .55

Page 9
1. 5/6 pie
2. 41/24 = 117/24 pizza
3. 5/9 cake
4. 1/6 candy bar
5. 37/24 = 113/24 pizza
6. 1/18 cake
7. 7/36 pizza

Page 10
Cloud Cover
10%–50%
50%–90%
90%

Thanksgiving Puzzle
Plymouth
Kite Factory
Tiger

Page 11
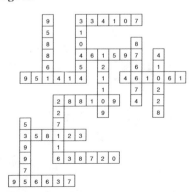

Page 12
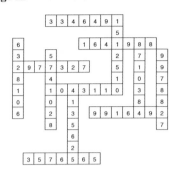

Page 13
1. 828
2. 697
3. 596
4. 1,522
5. 8,411
6. 1,578

Page 14
1. 18,941
2. 89,312
3. 42,133
4. 1,689,574

Page 15
1. $43,000
2. $38,500
3. $30,000
4. mean
5. mode
6. Answers will vary.
7. mode
8. Answers will vary.

Page 16
1. $a = 2$, $b = 4$, $c = 1$, $d = 3$
2. $e = 4$, $f = 10$, $g = 6$, $h = 1$
3. $i = 6$, $j = 1$, $k = 9$, $l = 3$
4. $m = 1$, $n = 3$, $o = 9$, $p = 7$
5. $q = 8$, $r = 1$, $s = 2$, $t = 3$
6. $u = 6$, $v = 3$, $w = 7$, $y = 1$
7. $a = 4$, $b = 10$, $c = 3$, $d = 2$
8. $e = 7$, $f = 6$, $g = 5$, $h = 9$
9. $i = 2$, $j = 3$, $k = 4$, $l = 8$
10. $a = 1$; $b = 6$, $c = 18$, $d = 19$
11. $e = 15$, $f = 7$, $g = 4$, $h = 17$
12. $i = 17$, $j = 10$, $k = 6$, $l = 16$

Page 17
1. $m = 19$, $n = 12$, $o = 16$, $p = 14$
2. $q = 17$, $r = 24$, $s = 36$, $t = 21$
3. $u = 96$, $v = 72$, $w = 16$, $y = 19$
4. $a = 82$, $b = 24$, $c = 11$, $d = 45$
5. $e = 33$, $f = 95$, $g = 19$, $h = 47$
6. $i = 95$, $j = 13$, $k = 10$, $l = 12$
7. $a = 4$, $b = 1$, $c = 9$, $d = 10$
8. $e = 5$, $f = 9$, $g = 2$, $h = 1$
9. $i = 8$, $j = 10$, $k = 2$, $l = 9$
10. $m = 7$, $n = 1$, $o = 2$, $p = 6$
11. $q = 7$, $r = 6$, $s = 5$, $t = 2$
12. $u = 9$, $v = 2$, $w = 10$, $y = 8$

Page 18
1. $a = 8$, $b = 6$, $c = 10$, $d = 1$
2. $e = 8$, $f = 5$, $g = 3$, $h = 1$
3. $i = 2$, $j = 6$, $k = 8$, $l = 4$
4. $a = 4$, $b = 3$, $c = 6$, $d = 2$
5. $e = 5$, $f = 1$, $g = 3$, $h = 15$
6. $i = 10$, $j = 4$, $k = 5$, $l = 2$
7. $m = 8$, $n = 3$, $o = 6$, $p = 4$
8. $q = 3$, $r = 5$, $s = 6$, $t = 10$
9. $u = 8$, $v = 3$, $w = 16$, $x = 6$
10. $a = 10$, $b = 25$, $c = 10$, $d = 4$
11. $e = 60$, $f = 40$, $g = 20$, $h = 30$
12. $i = 10$, $j = 20$, $k = 8$, $l = 25$

Page 19

		Monday	Tuesday	Wednesday	Thursday	Art Exhibit	Fair	Movie Premiere	Sporting Event
	Ana	O	X	X	X	X	O	X	X
	Dave	X	O	X	X	X	X	O	X
	Mario	X	X	X	O	X	X	X	O
	Steve	X	X	O	X	O	X	X	X

Ana went to the fair on Monday.

Dave went to the movie premiere on Tuesday.

Mario went to the sporting event on Thursday.

Steve went to the art exhibit on Wednesday.

Page 20

		5:45	6:00	6:15	6:30	6:45	Dessert	Rolls	Salad	Sodas	Spaghetti
	Betty	X	X	O	X	X	X	X	X	X	O
	Chaz	X	O	X	X	X	X	O	X	X	X
	Heidi	X	X	X	O	X	X	X	O	X	X
	Paul	O	X	X	X	X	O	X	X	X	X
	Roland	X	X	X	X	O	X	X	X	O	X

Betty arrived at 6:15 and brought the spaghetti.

Chaz arrived at 6:00 and brought the rolls.

Heidi arrived at 6:30 and brought the salad.

Paul arrived at 5:45 and brought the dessert.

Roland arrived at 6:45 and brought the sodas.

Page 21
$1, $2, $4, $8, $16, $32, $64

At the end of the week, Maureen has been paid $64.

$5, $10, $20, $40, $80, $160, $320, $640, $1,280, $2,560

John's paycheck will be $2,560

$10, $20, $40, $80, $320, $640, $1,280

It will take Henry at least 7 days to earn over a thousand dollars.

Page 23
1. $16,690.91
2. 10 hundred dollar bills
3. 50 ten dollar bills
4. 1,000 five dollar bills
5. 40 quarters
6. 400 quarters
7. 550,000,000 two dollar bills
8. 1,480,000,000 five dollar bills
9. 40,000 quarters

Answer Key

Page 24
1. California
2. Vermont, North Dakota
3. Vermont, North Dakota, Iowa
4. $86 billion dollars
5. Texas, Pennsylvania
6. $376 billion
7. 9.7%
8. 12.7%
9. 0.5%

Page 25
1. personal business, recreation
2. medical care
3. 1.4%
4. food, housing, tobacco
5. 26.4%
6. .83 trillion
7. .84 trillion
8. .96 trillion
9. .64 trillion

Page 26
(Answers on the chart may vary and be in a different order.)

green, blue, yellow, red
green, red, yellow, blue
green, red, blue, yellow
green, yellow, blue, red
green, yellow, red, blue
yellow, blue, red, green
yellow, blue, green, red
yellow, green, blue, red
yellow, green, red, blue
yellow, red, green, blue
yellow, red, blue, green

1. $3! = 3 \times 2 \times 1 = 6$
2. $4! = 4 \times 3 \times 2 \times 1 = 24$
3. $2! = 2 \times 1 = 2$

Page 27
(Answers on the chart may be in a different order than listed below.)

RYBOG	ROGYB
RYBGO	ROGBY
RYOGB	ROBYG
ROYGB	ROBGY
ROYBG	

1. 120 possible arrangements
2. $6! = 6 \times 5 \times 4 \times 3 \times 2 \times 1 = 720$
3. $7! = 7 \times 6 \times 5 \times 4 \times 3 \times 2 \times 1 = 5,040$

Page 28
1. $4 \times 3 = 12$
   white T with brown jeans
   white T with black jeans
   white T with purple jeans
   green T with brown jeans
   green T with black jeans
   green T with purple jeans
   blue T with black jeans
   blue T with purple jeans
   blue T with brown jeans
   yellow T with black jeans
   yellow T with purple jeans
   yellow T with brown jeans
2. $6 \times 2 = 12$
   white T with black jeans
   white T with brown jeans
   blue T with black jeans
   blue T with brown jeans
   green T with black jeans
   green T with brown jeans
   yellow T with black jeans
   yellow T with brown jeans
   red T with black jeans
   red T with brown jeans
   pink T with black jeans
   pink T with brown jeans
3. $9 \times 6 = 54$
4. $11 \times 12 = 132$
5. $2 \times 4 \times 3 = 24$
6. $2 \times 5 \times 4 \times 2 = 80$

Page 29
1. $3! = 3 \times 2 \times 1 = 6$
2. $4! = 4 \times 3 \times 2 \times 1 = 24$
3. $5! = 5 \times 4 \times 3 \times 2 \times 1 = 120$
4. $6! = 6 \times 5 \times 4 \times 3 \times 2 \times 1 = 720$
5. $4 - 3 = 1$
   $4!/1! = 4 \times 3 \times 2 \times 1 = 24$
6. $7 - 3 = 4$
   $7!/4! = 210$
   $7 \times 6 \times 5 \times 4 \times 3 \times 2 \times 1 = 5040$
   $4 \times 3 \times 2 \times 1 = 24$
   $5040 \div 24 = 210$
7. $9 - 4 = 5$
   $9!/5! = 3024$
   $9 \times 8 \times 7 \times 6 \times 5 \times 4 \times 3 \times 2 \times 1 = 362,880$
   $5 \times 4 \times 3 \times 2 \times 1 = 120$
   $362,880 \div 120 = 3024$

Page 30
1. Pam is 16, and Jane is 8.
2. Maurice is 15, Mark is 5, and Ray is 10.
3. Jerry is 2, Brent is 4, Fran is 1, and Charlotte is 8.
4. Steven is 9, Keith is 3, and Bryan is 6.
5. Juanita is 28 years old, and Benita is 14 years old.
6. Maria is 15 years old, and Raphael is 12 years old.
7. Noriko's grandmother was born in 1924, and her grandfather was born in 1920.
8. 82 days

Page 31

Frog Race

Frog 1 = 65 seconds

Frog 2 = 68 seconds

Frog 1 wins the race.

Bad Dogs

1:00 A.M.

Free Dinner

5 dinners

Race to Rescue

Joshua will reach his father first. At the first rate of 22 miles per hour, Benjamin's raft covers the distance of 40 miles in $40 \div 22 = 1.8$ hours. Adding the time for three delays, $3 \times 0.4 = 1.2$ hours, his total time is 3 hours.

Thirty percent of Joshua's 32-mile trail or ($32 \times 0.3 = 9.6$ miles) is steep, and at a rate of 8 miles per hour, he covers this steep section in $9.6 \div 8 = 1.2$ hours. At a rate of 15 miles per hour on the 22.4 mile flat section, Joshua covers this in $22.4 \div 15 = 1.5$ hours. His total time is 2.7 hours.

At her average rate of 5 miles per hour, Hannah covers her 14 mile mountain trail in $14 \div 5 = 2.8$ hours, but her rest time at the summit takes $10 \div 60$ or nearly 0.2 hours. So her total time, like Benjamin's, is 3 hours.

Their father rides Joshua's horse back to the village and treats the child.

Page 32

Clever Math Teachers

Mr. Ric Tangle and Ms. Py R. Square are in school while Mr. Perry Meter, Mr. Sol Ution, Ms. Dee Nominator, and Mr. Cal Culator are not.

Mr. Perry Meter is not at school. There are four 12's on one side of the equation and 5 on the other.

Mr. Ric Tangle is at school. The commutative property of numbers tells us that it doesn't matter what order the numbers are in when you multiply.

Ms. Py R. Square is at school. 50×30 would be 1,500 so 50×32 must be $> 1,000$.

Mr. Sol Ution is not at school. $1/4 + 1/4 = 1/2$, not 1/8.

Ms. Dee Nominator is not at school. The two numbers on the left of the equal sign are not quite the same as the two numbers on the right.

Mr. Cal Culator is not at school. If $33 + z = 107$, $z = 107 - 33$ which is 74, not 64.

At the Corner Store

The prices are: $1.20, $1.25, $1.50, and $3.16.

Page 33

Bare Feet

$12 - 7 = 5$ people in bare feet.

Two Trains Running

At time t, the distance the passenger train is from the terminal is $d = 50t$. At this same time, the distance the freight train is from the terminal is $d = 30(t + 1)$. The $t + 1$ is because at any given time t, the freight train has been traveling an hour longer than the second train. They pass each other when their two distances are the same or $30(t + 1) = 50t$. Solve for t to get 3/2 or 1.5 hours. The trains will pass each other after 1.5 hours.

Sheep or Kids?

There are two possible answers: 1 person and 2 sheep or 3 people and 1 sheep.

The Airplane and the Square

Side	Time (min.)
1	60
2	30
3	20
4	15

Answer Key

Total = 2 hours 5 minutes = 25/12 hours

Average speed = 400 miles ÷ (25/12) hours = 192 mph

Page 34
1. 5 mph
2. 25 mph
3. 5.5 mph
4. 8.7 mph
5. 2.4 mph
6. 250 miles
7. 840 miles
8. 11.25 miles
9. 585 miles
10. 37.1 miles
11. 30 hours
12. 3 hours
13. 10.5 hours
14. 65 hours
15. 8 hours

Page 35
Adam lives in #212.

Brandon lives in #213.

Gary lives in #210.

Louisa lives in #214.

Maria lives in #215.

Violet lives in #211.

Page 36
Adam sits in chair C.

Gary sits in chair D.

Louisa sits in chair B.

Brandon sits in chair E.

Maria sits in chair A.

Page 37
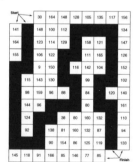

Page 38
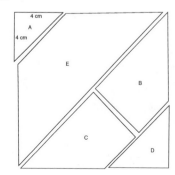

Page 39
Answers will vary.

Page 41
1. a. 1, 2, 3, 4, 5, 6, 8, 9, 10, 11
   b. 1, 2, 4, 6
   c. 1, 2
   d. 1, 2
2. a. 1, 2, 3, 4, 5, 6, 7, 9, 10, 11, 15, 16, 21, 25
   b. none
   c. 1
   d. none
3. a. 2, 3, 4, 6, 8, 9, 10, 12, 14, 15, 16
   b. 6, 12
   c. 4, 8, 12
   d. 12
4. a. 4, 6, 8, 12, 16, 18, 20, 24, 28, 30, 32, 36, 40
   b. 24
   c. 8, 16, 24, 32, 40
   d. 24
5. Answers will vary.

Page 42
1. a. 2, 3, 4, 5, 6, 8, 9, 12, 13, 14, 15, 17, 19, 28
   b. 3, 5, 6, 8, 9, 14, 15, 17, 19, 25, 36
   c. 2, 3, 4, 5, 6, 8, 9, 12, 13, 14, 15, 17, 19, 25, 28, 36
   d. 3, 9
   e. 3, 5, 9
   f. 3, 9
2. a. 1, 5, 7, 9, 10, 13, 15, 17, 18, 19, 20, 25, 28
   b. 1, 5, 7, 9, 10, 13, 14, 17, 18, 19, 25, 32
   c. 1, 5, 7, 9, 10, 13, 14, 15, 17, 18, 19, 20, 25, 28, 32
   d. 5, 7
   e. 5, 7, 19
   f. 5, 7
3. a. 5, 10, 15, 20, 25, 30, 35, 40, 50, 60, 70, 80, 90, 100, 110
   b. 5, 10, 15, 25, 35, 45, 50, 55, 80, 90, 100, 110
   c. 5, 10, 15, 20, 25, 30, 35, 40, 45, 50, 55, 60, 70, 80, 90, 100, 110
   d. 5, 10, 15
   e. 5, 15, 35
   f. 5, 15
4. a. 6, 12, 24, 30, 42, 48, 54, 66, 72, 96
   b. 6, 12, 24, 30, 36, 42, 48, 60, 72, 84, 96, 108
   c. 6, 12, 24, 30, 36, 42, 48, 54, 60, 66, 72, 84, 96, 108
   d. 6, 12, 30
   e. 6, 12
   f. 6, 12

Page 44
1. J = 8, A = 3
2. F = 1, I = 6
3. B = 5, F = 1
4. F = 1, G = 2
5. C = 7, J = 8
6. A = 3, C = 7, D = 9
7. H = 4, F = 1
8. B = 5, I = 6
9. D = 9, G = 2, A = 3
10. C = 7, J = 8, B = 5
11. B = 5
12. G = 2, E = 0
13. F = 1
14. A = 3
15. H = 4
16. R = 6, M = 0
17. U = 3, N = 5
18. R = 6, Z = 9, M = 0
19. W = 2, U = 3, X = 4
20. P = 7, Z = 9, Q = 8
21. V = 1, N = 5
22. Q = 8, W = 2, U = 3
23. P = 7, Z = 9, M = 0, V = 1
24. Z = 9, W = 2, U = 3, X = 4
25. Z = 9, M = 0
26. V = 1, M = 0
27. P = 7, Z = 9
28. X = 4, W = 2
29. U = 3, V = 1
30. R = 6, U = 3
31. W = 2
32. Q = 8, X = 4

Page 45
1. S = 4
2. P = 2
3. Y = 9
4. R = 5
5. C = 7
6. T = 8
7. C = 7, B = 6
8. P = 2, X = 3, C = 7
9. S = 4, R = 5, T = 8
10. P = 2, L = 0
11. C = 7, L = 0
12. B = 6, L = 0
13. M = 1, T = 8, C = 7
14. R = 5, X = 3, M = 1
15. C = 7, R = 5, M = 1, T = 8
16. A = 1
17. C = 9
18. E = 3, C = 9
19. J = 4, E = 3, D = 5, A = 1, C = 9, B = 2
20. G = 8, C = 9, F = 6
21. K = 7, F = 6, G = 8, B = 2
22. F = 6, G = 8
23. A = 1, B = 2, C = 9, D = 5
24. D = 5, J = 4, A = 1, F = 6
25. K = 7
26. D = 5